M000300314

GALE

CENGAGE Learning

Short Stories for Students, Volume 18

Project Editor: David Galens

Editorial: Anne Marie Hacht, Michelle Kazensky, Ira Mark Milne, Pam Revitzer, Kathy Sauer, Timothy J. Sisler, Jennifer Smith, Carol Ullmann

Research: Michelle Campbell, Sarah Genik, Tamara Notta

Permissions: Debra J. Freitas

Manufacturing: Stacy Melson

Imaging and Multimedia: Lezlie Light, Daniel William Newell, David G. Oblender, Kelly A. Quin, Luke Rademacher

Product Design: Pamela A. E. Galbreath

For more information, contact
Gale
27500 Drake Rd.
Farmington Hills, MI 48331-3535
Or you can visit our Internet site at
http://www.gale.com

While every effort has been made to ensure the reliability of the information presented in this

ISBN 0-7876-4270-3
ISSN 1092-7735

Printed in the United States of America
10 9 8 7 6 5 4 3 2 1

The Conversion of the Jews

Philip Roth 1959

Introduction

Philip Roth's "The Conversion of the Jews" was first published in 1959 in his first book, *Goodbye, Columbus, and Five Short Stories*. The book's novella and five short stories offended many Jewish Americans, who quickly lashed out at Roth for his unflattering depictions of Jewish Americans. However, most non-Jewish critics loved the book, and it received a 1960 National Book Award, an impressive achievement for a short-story collection, much less one from a new author. This polarized sentiment about Roth's works has persisted throughout his career, making him both controversial and adored. For critics who like Roth's writing, "The Conversion of the Jews" is viewed as a seminal story, which includes themes he has since examined in many other works.

The title of the story is derived from "To His Coy Mistress," a seventeenth-century poem by British poet Andrew Marvell in which the poet refers to the conversion of the Jews that some Christians believe will take place before the Last Judgment. The story was written and takes place in the 1950s, following the Holocaust of World War II, a time in which many Jews immigrated to the United States from Europe. Most Jews embraced assimilation into American culture but still attempted to maintain some degree of cultural solidarity. In the story, Ozzie Freedman, a Jewish teenager, questions the hypocrisy that he witnesses as a result of this solidarity and devotion to Jewish formalism. His rabbi's efforts to suppress Ozzie ultimately lead to Ozzie's escape onto the synagogue roof, where he achieves religious freedom by forcing the Jewish community to convert to Christianity. This story can be found in *American Short Story Masterpieces,* which was published by Laurel in 1987.

Author Biography

Roth was born in Newark, New Jersey, on March 19, 1933, into a working-class Jewish family. He attended Rutgers University (1950–1951), then transferred to Bucknell University, where he received his bachelor's degree in English in 1954. He received his master's degree in English from the University of Chicago in 1955; then he briefly joined the United States Army. However, within a year, he was discharged because of a back injury and returned to the University of Chicago. He did two years of doctoral work (1956–1957), working as an instructor at the same time. In 1957, he withdrew from the doctoral program, traveled for a summer in Europe, then moved to New York City. His experiences growing up as a Jewish American in a largely Jewish community have influenced many of his works, including his first work, *Goodbye, Columbus, and Five Short Stories* (1959), which included "The Conversion of the Jews." The book was awarded a National Book Award for fiction in 1960.

Over the next four decades, Roth published more than twenty books, including novels, two autobiographies, and a collection of essays. One book in particular, *Reading Myself and Others* (1975), addresses many of the controversial issues that surround Roth's satirical attacks on Jewish Americans. The book also addresses another controversy surrounding Roth's writing, the fact that he has repeatedly changed his style throughout his career. While most writers with long careers generally hone their writing skills in a certain style of writing, Roth has used a wide range of fiction styles, from tightly plotted novels to wildly experimental fables. In the past ten years, Roth has published six novels, including *Sabbath's Theater* (1995), which won a National Book Award for fiction the same year; *American Pastoral* (1997), which won both a National Book Award for fiction and the Pulitzer Prize for fiction in the same year; and *The Dying Animal* (2001). Roth lives and works in New York.

Plot Summary

"The Conversion of the Jews" starts with a theological conversation between Ozzie Freedman and his friend, Itzie Lieberman, two Jewish teenagers. Ozzie recounts an argument that he had that day with Rabbi Binder in Hebrew school at their synagogue, or Jewish place of worship. The rabbi had denounced the virgin birth of Jesus as impossible. Ozzie was confused because he had been taught to believe that God was all-powerful, which would mean that He could create a divine birth if He chose. Ozzie pushes the issue, and Rabbi Binder says he needs to speak with Ozzie's mother. This is the third time that Ozzie's widowed mother will have to come speak to the rabbi about Ozzie's religious questions. (The first two times were sparked by Ozzie's rebellion against the belief that Jews are the chosen people.) That night, Ozzie delays telling his mother about his day, waiting patiently while his mother performs her Sabbath candle-lighting ritual. Afterwards, he tells his mother why she needs to go meet with the rabbi the next day, and she slaps his face for the first time in his life.

The next day, during free-discussion time, Ozzie asks his previous question about why God cannot do anything He chooses to do, then he insults the rabbi by attacking his knowledge of God. The rabbi smacks Ozzie's face, giving him a bloody nose. Ozzie curses the rabbi and escapes to the roof of the synagogue. Yakov Blotnik, the old custodian at the synagogue, calls the fire department, thinking that the firemen will get Ozzie off the roof as they once did a cat. The fire engines arrive, drawing a larger crowd in the process. A fireman asks Ozzie if he is going to jump, and Ozzie says he will, and then he runs around to different parts of the roof, making the firemen follow him on the ground with their safety net. The rabbi gets down on his knees and pleads with Ozzie not to jump, while Ozzie's friends tell him to jump. Amid this commotion, Ozzie's mother arrives and pleads with Ozzie not to jump. Ozzie carefully considers whether he should commit suicide. He tells everybody to kneel, and they do, assuming the Gentile, or non-Jewish, posture of prayer. Ozzie makes the rabbi and the assembled crowd say that they believe God can do anything, including making a child without intercourse, and that they believe in Jesus Christ. After this, Ozzie starts to cry, and he makes his mother and the rabbi say that they will not ever hit anybody over religious matters, like they did him. The entire crowd repeats this statement, then Ozzie jumps safely off the roof into the firemen's net.

Rabbi Marvin Binder

Rabbi Binder is Ozzie's teacher at the Hebrew school who constantly punishes Ozzie for his religious questions, which the rabbi sees as deliberately insolent behavior. The rabbi believes in order and does not like to have his explanations questioned. When Ozzie asks him about the possibility of Jesus Christ's virgin birth, the rabbi says that Jesus was an historical figure, not a divine one. Ozzie says the rabbi knows nothing about God, and Rabbi Binder tries to lightly slap Ozzie on the face, but ends up giving Ozzie a bloody nose. Ozzie curses the rabbi and escapes onto the roof. The rabbi tries to be firm with Ozzie, commanding him to come down off the roof. This does not work and, at several points, it looks like Ozzie is going to fall or jump off the roof to his death. The rabbi falls to his knees, pleading with Ozzie to come down, then crying. At Ozzie's request, he says that he believes God can make a child without intercourse, he believes in Jesus Christ, and he will never hit anybody again over a religious matter.

Yakov Blotnik

Yakov Blotnik is the synagogue's aged custodian, who calls the fire department. He is only interested in whether situations are good or bad for

Jews. Ozzie believes that Blotnik's constant praying is meaningless, since Blotnik appears not even to know the meaning of what he is saying anymore.

Mrs. Freedman

Mrs. Freedman is Ozzie Freedman's widowed mother. Mrs. Freedman is a devout Jew and reverently observes Jewish rituals such as the Sabbath. She is distressed that she has to keep going to see Rabbi Binder about Ozzie's behavior and slaps Ozzie's face after he tells her she must do so again. This is the first time that she has slapped Ozzie. When Mrs. Freedman comes to the synagogue for her appointment with the rabbi, she sees Ozzie on the roof and pleads with him not to jump. At Ozzie's request, she gets down on her knees and says that she believes God can make a child without intercourse, she believes in Jesus Christ, and she will never hit anybody again over a religious matter.

Oscar Freedman

Oscar Freedman is a thirteen-year-old Jewish boy whose persistent questions about the validity of Judaism eventually lead him to escape the classroom and go onto the synagogue roof. Oscar, known throughout most of the story as Ozzie, is an earnest young man who wants to understand his religion. As a result, he reads the Hebrew book very slowly, trying to comprehend each word, and questions his religion in ways that others do not dare. These actions constantly get Ozzie in trouble with Rabbi Binder, who feels that Ozzie is being deliberately insolent. Ozzie is particularly troubled by the fact that Jews do not acknowledge the possibility of Jesus' divine birth, even though Jews believe that God is all-powerful. Ozzie persists in his question about this issue, and then he says that Rabbi Binder knows nothing about God. The rabbi hits Ozzie, who then curses Rabbi Binder. Ozzie escapes onto the synagogue roof and ignores the rabbi's commands to come down. The fire department comes, and Ozzie makes them move back and forth, shadowing his movements as he runs from one end of the roof to the other, threatening to jump. While Rabbi Binder pleads with Ozzie to come down safely, Itzie Lieberman and the other children chant for Ozzie to jump and kill himself. Ozzie threatens to commit suicide unless his mother kneels. Then, Ozzie makes the largely Jewish crowd kneel, admit that God can make a child without intercourse, and profess their belief in Jesus Christ. After this mass conversion, Ozzie starts to cry and makes them promise that they will never hit anybody over a religious matter. Finally, he jumps safely into the firemen's net.

Itzie Lieberman

Itzie Lieberman, Ozzie's best friend, initially criticizes Ozzie's outspoken behavior but later encourages Ozzie to jump off the synagogue roof. In class, while Ozzie persists in asking Rabbi Binder about the possibility of Jesus' virgin birth,

Itzie is content with making gestures behind the rabbi's back. However, after Ozzie goes up on the synagogue roof, Itzie becomes more outspoken. While the rabbi pleads with Ozzie not to jump, Itzie starts chanting for Ozzie to jump and kill himself, inspiring other children to chant as well.

Ozzie

See Oscar Freedman

Hypocrisy

Ozzie is a truth-seeker who does not deal well with factual inconsistencies, especially in his religion. He is passionate about Judaism and deeply respectful of its beliefs and rituals. When his mother lights candles on the Sabbath, he picks the ringing phone off the hook but does not answer it; instead, he holds it "muffled to his chest." He does not want anything to disturb his mother's ritual: "When his mother lit candles Ozzie felt there should be no noise; even breathing, if you could manage it, should be softened." However, as much as he strives to be a respectful Jew, he has problems claiming allegiance with any religion that supports hypocrisy —the act of claiming to be something that one is not or believing in something that one knows is not true. Ozzie knows that Jews believe in the all-powerful nature of God. As a result, he is surprised when the Jewish elders to whom he looks for guidance—his mother and his rabbi—fail to acknowledge even the possibility of Jesus' divine birth. Ozzie is even more shocked when his mother and rabbi hit him as a result of his attempts to point out this hypocrisy.

Ozzie sees evidence of this hypocrisy in other areas of the Jewish life. He notices Yakov Blotnik, the seventy-one-year-old custodian, who constantly mumbles prayers to himself that he does not seem to understand. Ozzie believes that it is more important to understand one's prayers than to mouth them ritualistically without understanding. Ozzie follows the same belief when he reads slowly from the Hebrew book in order to increase his comprehension. But doing so gets him in trouble with Rabbi Binder: "Ozzie said he could read faster but that if he did he was sure not to understand what he was reading." However, the rabbi does not care whether Ozzie can understand. As far as the rabbi is concerned, the important thing is that Ozzie follows the rules.

Media Adaptations

- *Goodbye, Columbus, and Five Other Short Stories* was adapted as an unabridged audio file by Audio Literature. It is available on the Web at www.audible.com and features several narrators, including Theodore Bikel and Harlan Ellison.

- *Goodbye, Columbus* was released by Paramount Pictures in 1969 as a feature film entitled *Goodbye Columbus*. The film, which was directed by Larry Peerce, featured Richard Benjamin, Ali MacGraw, and Jack Klugman. It is available on VHS from Paramount Home Video.

Freedom

When Ozzie asks questions about his religion, he is not trying to be "deliberately simple-minded and a wise guy," as the rabbi assumes. He is earnestly trying to understand his religion. Nevertheless, in his quest for truth, he comes up against a restrictive wall of religious authority, represented mainly by Rabbi Binder. On the surface, the rabbi encourages students to ask him questions. However, the students also witness the rabbi's "soul-battering" of Ozzie after Ozzie tries to question the idea of reading faster at the expense of comprehension. For them, the rabbi's actions speak louder than his words: "Consequently when free-discussion time rolled around none of the students felt too free." The students do not ask any questions, and the silence is filled only with Blotnik's rote, uninspired prayers. This detail underscores the fact that what Rabbi Binder really wants is conformity.

Blotnik is an obedient Jew, one who adheres totally to his faith. Roth states: "For Yakov Blotnik life had fractionated itself simply: things were either good-for-the-Jews or no-good-for-the-Jews." When he witnesses Ozzie up on the roof, Blotnik surveys the situation and sees that nobody outside of the synagogue is watching, so "it-wasn't-so-bad-for-the-Jews. But the boy had to come down immediately, before anybody saw." Blotnik is concerned more with his religion's reputation or image than with Ozzie's safety.

However, Ozzie has no intention of coming down from the roof, at least not right away. He escapes to the roof to get away from his rabbi but soon realizes that his position on the roof gives him great power. When Rabbi Binder commands Ozzie to come down, Ozzie can see that the rabbi is bluffing, because he has no way of making Ozzie follow his order. "It was the attitude of a dictator, but one—the eyes confessed all—whose personal valet had spit neatly in his face." When Ozzie realizes that he is in charge, not the rabbi, he starts "to feel the meaning of the word control: he felt Peace and he felt Power." Once Ozzie realizes that the crowd also thinks he is going to kill himself, and the rabbi and his mother do not want him to do so, he gains even more power. He uses the freedom of his newfound power to once again address his question about the possibility of Jesus' virgin birth. This time, he takes it one step further, by forcing the assembled crowd—including the rabbi, his mother, and even Blotnik—to say they believe God can do anything, they believe in the possibility of a virgin birth, and they believe in Jesus. By forcing the crowd to acknowledge his beliefs, Ozzie beats the system of religious authority and achieves the freedom that he has been seeking.

Topics for Further Study

- Christianity has a long history of attempting to convert non-Christians. Jews, on the other hand, do not usually try to convert others to their religion, although converts are generally welcome. Research the steps required to convert to Judaism and create a diagram that depicts these steps. Include relevant artwork, photos, quotes, or other sources that illustrate each of these steps.

- Choose any example from history in which a mass of people was converted to Christianity, either by choice or against their will. Write a short overview of this event, discussing where and when this mass conversion took place, whether the converted people had a choice in their conversion, and what long-term effects the event had.

- Using a standard calendar, plot all of the Christian and Jewish holidays. Write a short description of each holiday, including its history and traditional rituals. Also, discuss the differences between a standard calendar and the Jewish calendar.

- Research the Jewish bar mitzvah ceremony. Imagine being a Jewish boy or girl going through your own bar or bat mitzvah. Write a journal entry that describes what the bar or bat mitzvah is like, using research to support your ideas.

Irreverence

The story raises the issue of what constitutes irreverence, or lack of respect, for one's religion. Characters in the story variously interpret the concept. The rabbi thinks that Ozzie's questions are deliberately disrespectful. He is shocked when Ozzie, frustrated that he is not getting answers, tells him: "You don't know! You don't know anything about God!" He is even more astounded when Ozzie curses him after he smacks Ozzie for this comment. "Ozzie screamed, 'You bastard, you bastard!' and broke for the classroom door." For Rabbi Binder, these are all clear signs of irreverence. As for Ozzie, he does not think his questions are irreverent, since he is asking them out of a genuine desire to understand. However, even Ozzie is surprised that he has cursed his rabbi and wonders whether he is still himself—"For a thirteen-year-old who had just labeled his religious leader a bastard, twice, it was not an improper question." However, upon further examination, Ozzie believes that he is not being irreverent. On the contrary, he feels that, by taking a stand against religious hypocrisy, he is more reverent than his rabbi or any other conformist Jew. In fact, he feels so comfortable with his actions that he briefly considers the possibility of jumping off the roof and dying for his cause. Finally, there is the case of Itzie, who is deliberately irreverent but who practices a passive form of disrespect. Itzie has seen Ozzie's outspoken behavior get him in trouble to the point where Ozzie's mother has to come talk to the rabbi. Itzie, who is irreverent for the thrill of misbehaving not because he has serious issues with his faith, does not think getting in trouble is worth it. "Itzie preferred to keep *his* mother in the kitchen; he settled for behind-the-back subtleties such as gestures, faces, snarls and other less delicate barnyard noises."

Style

Satire

Satire is a form of criticism that makes its point through biting irony and ridicule. Satire can be more effective than direct discussion because satire leaves a lasting image. In the story, Roth's satirical target is Jewish formalism in the 1950s, particularly in Jewish communities like the one depicted in the story. In this community, Jews take to ludicrous and dispassionate extremes the belief that they are God's chosen ones. For example, Ozzie's mother studies a newspaper article describing a plane crash and only declares the accident a tragedy when she sees that eight of the victims have distinctly Jewish names. Roth satirizes this Jewish community in other ways, too, such as in Rabbi Binder's insistence that Ozzie read fast from the Hebrew book, even though he does not understand the words. Of course, the ultimate satire is the fact that the rabbi, a representative of Jewish religious authority, refuses to acknowledge the possibility of a virgin birth, even though this refusal means denying the fact that his Jewish God is all-powerful.

Imagery

Unlike the Jewish community in the story, which Roth portrays as very closed-minded, Ozzie is an independent thinker who views his world in an expressive way. Nothing is boring for Ozzie. His mind, which depicts even simple acts and situations as vivid images, influences the narration. The imagery in the story is particularly expressive when it applies to Ozzie's religious beliefs. For example, he likes watching his mother perform the ritual of lighting candles: "When his mother lit the candles she would move her two arms slowly towards her, dragging them through the air, as though persuading people whose minds were half made up." Ozzie is enthralled by the spiritual nature of this simple yet meaningful ceremony. The power of this image makes him think that his mother will support his religious inquiry into the possible divine birth of Jesus. Says the narrator, "when she lit candles she looked like … a woman who knew momentarily that God could do anything." For this reason, he is crushed when his mother hits him for asking his question in class.

Ozzie thinks he is going to receive an even harsher punishment from the rabbi when he curses him and escapes onto the synagogue's roof. Ozzie locks the trap door and sits on it to prevent the rabbi from coming after him. However, Ozzie is still tied to the traditional Jewish belief that one should never disrespect a rabbi, and so he imagines violent consequences. As the narrator notes, "any instant he was certain that Rabbi Binder's shoulder would fling it open, splintering the wood into shrapnel and catapulting his body into the sky." When this does not happen, Ozzie begins to realize that his religion is not as powerful as he had assumed. Although this gives him a sense of power, it also puts him in a state of confusion, since he does not know where to go for guidance for serious issues such as whether he should die for his religious beliefs. In one of the most expressive images in the story, Ozzie looks to the heavens for answers: "Yearningly, Ozzie wished he could rip open the sky, plunge his hands through, and pull out the sun; and on the sun, like a coin, would be stamped JUMP or DON'T JUMP."

Symbolism

Some of the images in the story also have symbolic meanings. A symbol is a physical object, action, or gesture that represents an abstract concept, without losing its original identity. A symbol can be local, with a meaning that is dependent upon the context of the story. It can also be universal, with a meaning that remains the same regardless of its context. The most prominent examples of local symbols in the story are the last names of Ozzie and the rabbi. Ozzie's last name is "Freedman," which symbolizes his quest for religious freedom, in which his rebellion makes him a freed man. His main opponent is Rabbi "Binder," who constantly tries to restrict Ozzie's religious inquiries and bind him to formal Jewish doctrine.

The story also contains several universal symbols. One that evolves throughout the story is connected to the crowd of Jewish children that gathers on the street outside the synagogue to watch Ozzie on the roof. When Ozzie first observes this crowd, the narrator describes it as follows: "In little jagged starlike clusters his friends stood around Rabbi Binder." Whenever a star is used in conjunction with Jews or Judaism, it usually refers to the Magen of David. This six-pointed star, which is located on the flag of Israel—the world's only Jewish state—is a recognized symbol of Jewish solidarity. When the children form themselves into star-shaped groups around the rabbi, the shape suggests the idea of cultural unity. However, as Ozzie realizes that he has the power to rebel against his religion, the children in the crowd follow his example, starting with Itzie. "Itzie broke off his point of the star and courageously, with the inspiration not of a wise guy but of a disciple, stood alone." The use of the word "disciple," a term generally used to refer to the followers of Jesus in his lifetime, underscores even more the religious significance of Itzie's defiant gesture. As more children follow suit, the star disintegrates, a clear symbol of religious rebellion.

The Attempted Annihilation of the Jews

To understand the historical context of the 1950s, when Roth wrote the story and when the story takes place, one must first look at the mass killing known as the Holocaust. During World War II (1939–1945), the German Nazi regime carried out a plan of genocide known as The Final Solution. The Nazis intended to wipe out European Jewry. They nearly succeeded. Prior to World War II, approximately nine million Jews lived in Europe. Of these, roughly six million Jews, or two-thirds, had died by the war's end.

The Migration of the Jews

Following the defeat of the Nazis, many European Jews could no longer face life in Europe and became part of a mass migration to other countries. In 1948, the Jewish state of Israel, the first Jewish state in nearly two thousand years, was formed in Palestine. Some European Jews chose to migrate to this new Jewish homeland. However, Israel was economically disadvantaged and experienced near-constant hostility from its Arab neighbors, so it was not an attractive choice for many European Jews, who had just been through a war. For those who did not go to Israel, a new opportunity presented itself in the United States. Jews had been living there since its founding, but anti-Semitism was prevalent in the States until and even during World War II. When the gruesome details of the Holocaust came to light, American anti-Semitic feelings dissipated.

The Assimilation of the Jews

Now that Jews were more welcome in the United States, they came in large numbers in the late 1940s and the 1950s, eager to take advantage of American freedom and other opportunities. The Jewish community as a whole, recognizing that Jewish prosperity in the States hinged on the ability to blend in, encouraged assimilation into American culture. The segregation of distinctly Jewish communities, which had been practiced in Europe, was now seen as a barrier to success. The rapid development of U.S. suburbs after World War II helped Jews assimilate rapidly. Except in certain neighborhoods where anti-Semitic tensions still existed, Jews moved next door to non-Jewish neighbors and formed multi-faith friendships.

The Education of the Jews

One area in which Jews, especially children, were rapidly assimilated was in their education. Traditionally, Jews receive extensive education in their faith from both their parents and the community. To help their children fit in as

Americans, many Jewish parents sent their children to public schools. As a result, most Jewish children received their Jewish education in Hebrew school, a supplementary schooling that took place in the afternoons after the public schools let out.

Critical Overview

Roth's critical reputation for "The Conversion of the Jews" is the same as for the rest of his works: sharply divided. Sanford Pinsker sums it up best in his 1984 entry on Roth for the *Dictionary of Literary Biography:* "His readers tend to have strong attachment to one end or the other of the evaluative yardstick, which is to say, people either love his fiction or they hate it. Gray areas are rare indeed." This trend began with Roth's first book, *Goodbye, Columbus, and Five Short Stories.* Much of the Jewish community, critics and readers alike, were shocked and outraged at Roth's negative or unflattering depictions of American Jews. As Pinsker says, the book "made it clear that Roth was a force to be reckoned with." Pinsker also notes that the book "changed the ground rules by which one wrote about American-Jewish life."

Compare & Contrast

- **1950s:** Following the Holocaust during World War II, which kills an estimated six million Jews, many European Jews emigrate to other countries such as Israel and the United States. In 1957, due to this migration, the United States attains the world's largest Jewish population.

Today: The majority of the world's estimated thirteen million Jews live in either the United States, which hosts almost six million Jews, or Israel, which hosts almost five million Jews.

- **1950s:** Most American Jews encourage assimilation with American culture as a way to get ahead and make a better life for themselves.

  Today: The biggest problem facing American Jewry is the loss of its Jewish identity as a result of assimilation into American culture. Judaism, like other major religions, is in a state of flux as it attempts to reconcile secular issues with religious traditions.

- **1950s:** Intermarriage is frowned upon, and a mere 6 percent of Jewish marriages are to non-Jews.

  Today: More than 50 percent of all Jewish marriages are to non-Jews.

Most critics who like Roth's work have also liked "The Conversion of the Jews." Many of them note the story's use of themes that Roth revisits in much of his work. Even those who do not like the story, like Peter L. Cooper, agree that it is one of Roth's seminal works. In his 1991 entry on Roth for

American Writers, Cooper notes: "Although marred by a simplistic treatment of good and bad, a strained resolution, and a heavy-handed underscoring of 'message,' the story presents issues that pervade the later work." As Judith Paterson Jones and Guinevera A. Nance note in their 1981 book, *Philip Roth,* these issues include "the difficulties of communication in a world in which materialism has replaced spirituality" and "representation of the individual in a society that values 'normality' and conformity more than the development of the individual."

Of course, these are generic themes. Many critics are more specific and note Roth's application of these themes to Jewish life, which has continued to outrage much of the Jewish-American community. However, as Naseeb Shaheen notes in his 1976 article for *Studies in Short Fiction,* this negative criticism has not affected sales. Says Shaheen, "the fact that his works on Jewish themes have been by far the most successful of all his works indicates where his genius truly lies." As Roth has come under repeated fire from the Jewish community, some critics who like Roth's work have explored answers to Jews' questions about why Roth would depict them in such a manner. In his overview of "The Conversion of the Jews" in *Reference Guide to Short Fiction,* Steven Goldleaf answers the question, posed by members of the Jewish community, of why Roth would portray Jewish people "as small-minded bigots who suppress Ozzie's inquiries." Goldleaf responds: "The reason is the same for both Roth's affront and for Ozzie's: because, by restricting free discussion, the community harms itself while claiming to defend itself."

Likewise, in their 1990 book, *Understanding Philip Roth,* Murray Baumgarten and Barbara Gottfried offer some historical background of actual events in the Jewish community at the time, which support Roth's satirical attacks in the story: "Like many Jewish communal leaders in the 1950s Rabbi Binder spends the greater part of his energies in separating what is Jewish from what is non-Jewish." Shaheen agrees, noting specifically the inability of Rabbi Binder and others in the story to acknowledge the possibility of Jesus' virgin birth. Says Shaheen in 1976, two decades after the story was written: "The tenacity with which this conviction is held in some Jewish circles is disquieting."

What Do I Read Next?

- Saul Bellow's *The Adventures of Augie March* (1953) concerns the title character, a young Jewish American in a working-class Chicago neighborhood, who is forced to embark upon a number of odd jobs during the Great Depression. Despite all of his negative experiences, Augie fights to remain optimistic and attempts to make sense of the world by seeking a worthwhile fate.

- Since the Holocaust, a number of prominent Catholic and Protestant religious leaders have made public statements expressing remorse at the Christian mistreatment of Jews and have also expressed the desire to recognize the validity of Judaism. *Christianity in Jewish Terms* (2000), a collection of essays by Tikva Frymer-Kensky and more than thirty other Jewish and Christian scholars, opens a dialogue about the similarities and differences between the two faiths.

- The essays in Richard J. Israel's *The Kosher Pig: And Other Curiosities of Modern Jewish Life* (1993) explore the difficulty of adhering to traditional Jewish beliefs and practices in a modern world. Israel explores his many topics with humor and insight and offers such eclectic tips as how to survive a Yom Kippur fast with the least amount of discomfort and how to keep a *yarmulke*—or skullcap—on a bald head.

- In Bernard Malamud's *The Assistant* (1957), Frankie Alpine, an Italian-American street thug, gets a job working for a humble Jewish-American grocer, Morris Bober. Morris cannot modernize his traditional Jewish beliefs, even though his inability to change threatens his family's economic survival. Meanwhile, Frankie falls in love with Morris's daughter and is forced to question his own moral and religious beliefs.

- In Roth's novel *The Ghost Writer* (1979), Nathan Zuckerman is a young Jewish-American author who is in love with the literary classics. Zuckerman's father does not see the value in his son's story, which portrays Jews in a negative fashion, and Zuckerman seeks out his literary idol, E. I. Lonoff, for guidance. During an evening at Lonoff's rural home, Zuckerman explores the complex nature of a writer's moral responsibility to both art and society.

- In *Reading Myself and Others* (1975), Roth collects a number of his previously published articles and essays. These include commentary on his works, his reasons for writing about Jews in ways that are sometimes viewed as disparaging by members of the Jewish community, and various aspects of Roth's life.

Sources

Baumgarten, Murray, and Barbara Gottfried, *Understanding Philip Roth,* University of South Carolina Press, 1990, p. 45.

Cooper, Peter L., "Philip Roth," in *American Writers,* Supplement 3, Vol. 2, Charles Scribner's Sons, 1991, pp. 401–29.

Goldleaf, Steven, "'The Conversion of the Jews': Overview," in *Reference Guide to Short Fiction,* 1st ed., edited by Noelle Watson, St. James Press, 1994.

Jones, Judith Paterson, and Guinevera A. Nance, "Good Girls and Boys Gone Bad," in *Philip Roth,* Frederick Ungar Publishing Company, 1981, pp. 9–85.

Pinsker, Sanford, "Philip Roth," in *Dictionary of Literary Biography,* Vol. 28: *Twentieth-Century American-Jewish Fiction Writers,* edited by Daniel Walden, Gale Research, 1984, pp. 264–75.

Roth, Philip, "The Conversion of the Jews," in *American Short Story Masterpieces,* edited by Raymond Carver and Tom Jenks, Laurel, 1987, pp. 440–55, originally published in *Goodbye, Columbus, and Five Short Stories,* Houghton, 1959.

Shaheen, Naseeb, "Binder Unbound, or, How Not to Convert the Jews," in *Studies in Short Fiction,* Vol.

13, No. 3, Summer 1976, pp. 376–78.

Further Reading

Brodkin, Karen, *How Jews Became White Folks: And What That Says about Race in America,* Rutgers University Press, 1998.

> Brodkin explores her own racial status as a Jewish American and discusses how Jews have shifted from the non-white to the white category in the American social consciousness. She also applies this discussion to the greater issue of how racial-ethnic backgrounds help to define social identities in the United States.

Cooper, Alan, *Philip Roth and the Jews,* State University of New York Press, 1996.

> Cooper examines and dispels the common impression that Roth is either a self-hating Jew or a writer bent on making fun of the Jewish community. Cooper reviews Roth's life and works and compares the author's experiences to the experiences of Jewish Americans in general.

Dershowitz, Alan M., *The Vanishing American Jew: In Search of Jewish Identity for the Next Century,* Little, Brown and Company, 1997.

Dershowitz says that modern Jewish Americans face a different challenge than previous generations, which fought against an anti-Semitic attitude that has largely disappeared. Instead, today's Jewish Americans, who have been widely assimilated into American culture, stand to lose their Jewish identity through the increase in intermarriage and the lapse of Jewish practices. Dershowitz proposes some steps to ensure that a permanent loss of identity does not happen.

Heilman, Samuel C., *Portrait of American Jews: The Last Half of the Twentieth Century,* University of Washington Press, 1995.

Heilman draws from his dual background as sociologist and Jewish Studies professor to demonstrate the sociological changes that have taken place in the Jewish-American community since the 1950s.

Robinson, George, *Essential Judaism: A Complete Guide to Beliefs, Customs, and Rituals,* Pocket Books, 2000.

Robinson offers an up-to-date, one-volume overview of Jewish practices and beliefs. Written in an accessible style, the book includes several sidebars that highlight specific aspects of Judaism, answer the most commonly asked questions, and explore current controversies.